"Our challenge isn't so much to teach children about the natural world, but to find ways to nurture and sustain the instinctive connections they already carry."

Quote by Terry Krautwurst
author of "Nature Smart: Awesome Projects to Make with Mother Nature's Help"

Mother Nature Knows...

Written and Illustrated by Kelly Foxton

Dedicated with love to my children

Laine, Teague and Gavin

Text and illustrations copyright 2013 by Kelly Foxton.

ISBN 978-0-9919131-0-7

www.naturebooks4kids.com

To order additional copies and for all other inquiries, please write to:

Kelly Foxton, Bear River, Nova Scotia, Canada B0S1B0

kfoxton@yahoo.com

Mother Nature Knows that

all of Her children...

...have a very special place

in this World.

Mother Nature knows...

...that sometimes we have to
stand apart from the rest...

...in order to be our best.

Mother Nature knows...

...that when we pay attention to the beautiful things in this world...

...we inspire others to do
the same.

Mother Nature knows...

...that even the smallest of us...

...has a very important job to do.

Mother Nature knows...

...that if we're still enough...

...and quiet enough...

...new things will be revealed.

Mother Nature knows...

...that if we treat all of Her children the way we would like them to treat us...

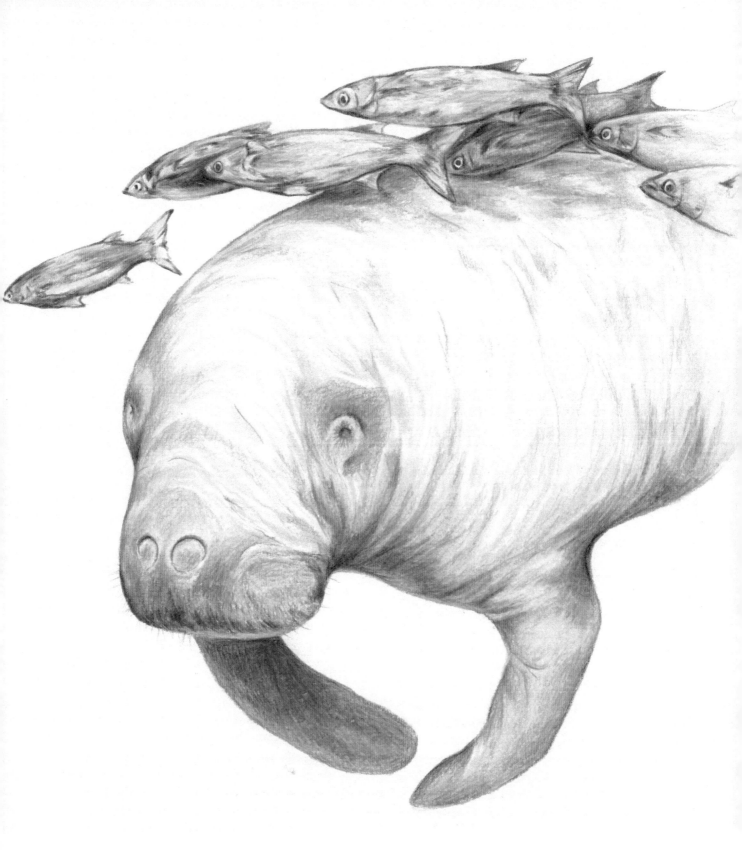

...we will live happily together for a
very long time.

Mother Nature knows
that deep in our hearts...

...we know too.

"Efforts to teach children to love and respect nature are priceless ... I hope this new generation will look after our planet better than we have." -David Suzuki www.davidsuzuki.org

Mother Nature freely gives us everything we need to live happy, healthy lives on this beautiful planet Earth. All She asks in return is for us to show Her and all Her children the same love and respect that we would want them to show us. By spending time in nature observing the animals and the natural world, we can learn a great deal about ourselves, each other, and the many gifts this planet has to offer.

The following notes are meant to offer readers a glimpse into my own personal understanding of the co-relation between the universal nature teachings presented in this book and the animals that inspired each illustration. In some cases I've also shared links to websites however, these links are by no means meant to be an exhaustive list. There truly are more fabulous resources to be found out there than could possibly fit into a book of this size and I encourage readers to do their own independent research into current issues facing our Mother Earth.

May your journey inspire you to listen to the wisdom in your own heart, to join in the effort to make changes for the better, and to be part of the next generation that will indeed "look after our planet better than we have." Children of the Earth, Walk Softly.

Wishing you many blessings, Kelly Foxton

"Mother Nature knows that all of Her children have a very special place in this world."

Polar bears, arctic wolves and caribou are just a few of the amazing creatures that make their home in the Arctic. The Inuit people have coexisted in harmony with these animals for thousands of years. Today, habitat loss is one of the major issues threatening their survival and way of life. The challenges that our two-legged and four-legged brothers and sisters of the north face have a lot to teach us about respecting the delicate balance that exists in all of earths natural places.
For more information about life in the Arctic check out http://oceansnorth.org/arctic-ecology

"Mother Nature knows that sometimes we have to stand apart from the rest in order to be our best."

Cougars are extremely powerful, solitary creatures. These majestic masters of camouflage are commonly found in western Canada but have been sighted as far east as Nova Scotia. Thirty five years ago the Eastern cougar was declared an "endangered" species but reports of recent sightings keep hope alive that some still remain in eastern Canada's dwindling forests. Cougars teach us about honouring our individuality, and the value of thinking for ourselves and making time in our lives for quiet reflection.
Read more about cougars at http://www.naturecanada.ca/endangered_know_our_species_ecougar.asp

"Mother Nature knows that when we pay attention to the beautiful things in this world we inspire others to do the same."

Butterflies and hummingbirds are among the beauty-seeking creatures that help bees and other pollinating insects find the most brilliantly coloured blossoms. In doing so, they play a key role in insuring the regeneration of the strongest, healthiest plants.

By following Nature's example, we too can be "beauty seekers" and inspire others to help make this world a happier, healthier place for everyone.

"Mother Nature knows that even the smallest of us has a very important job to do."

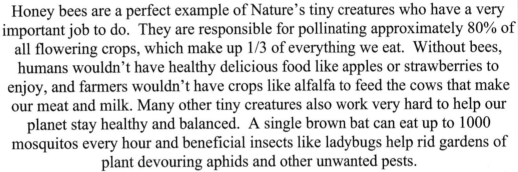

Honey bees are a perfect example of Nature's tiny creatures who have a very important job to do. They are responsible for pollinating approximately 80% of all flowering crops, which make up 1/3 of everything we eat. Without bees, humans wouldn't have healthy delicious food like apples or strawberries to enjoy, and farmers wouldn't have crops like alfalfa to feed the cows that make our meat and milk. Many other tiny creatures also work very hard to help our planet stay healthy and balanced. A single brown bat can eat up to 1000 mosquitos every hour and beneficial insects like ladybugs help rid gardens of plant devouring aphids and other unwanted pests.

Thinking about Nature's tiny creatures helps remind us that we too are perfectly designed to do our own unique and very important jobs. No matter how small we may think we are, we are big enough to make a difference!

Read more about tiny, helpful creatures at
http://www.organicgardening.com/learn-and-grow/meet-beneficial-insects
http://www.pollinationcanada.ca/
http://www.batcon.org/

"Mother Nature knows that if we're still enough and quiet enough new things will be revealed."

Have you ever been scurrying around looking for something only to find that what you were searching for was right there the whole time? - you just couldn't see it because you were too busy rushing around to notice. Mother Nature knows that a healthy balance of busyness and stillness is very important.

The animals learn the value of stillness at a very young age. Mother deer, rabbits and other ground dwellers of the forest hide their babies in thick brush to protect them from predators. The babies know to be very still and silent while they wait. Even larger adult animals practice the art of stillness. Creatures of the forest are normally very shy and can sense us coming long before we see or hear them. They are capable of staying very alert while standing still and quiet for long periods of time. Because of this, humans have been known to walk within feet of wolves, deer and other amazing creatures without realizing it.

Spending quiet time in nature helps us become more alert and observant and reminds us that sometimes the answers to life's most difficult questions lay not in the "doing", but in the "un-doing"…in the stillness and the silence that enables us to hear our inner voice and follow the wisdom of our hearts.

"Mother Nature knows that if we treat all of Her children the way we would like them to treat us we will live happily together for a very long time."

Every day the lives of sea turtles and manatees are negatively impacted by careless human behaviour. The *Save the Manatee Club* reported that the number one cause of manatee deaths in 2012 was watercraft collision, and the *Canadian Sea Turtle network* reported that the number one threat to sea turtles in the wild is drowning in commercial fishing nets.

The challenges these animals face in the wild have a lot to teach us about learning to ask ourselves this very important question before we act: "Would I want someone to do this to me?" If the answer is NO, then we know it's time to stop and reassess our decisions.

For more information on how you can help make the world a better place for manatees and sea turtles, check out the following links:

Canadian Sea Turtle "Free the Leatherback" initiative
http://www.freetheleatherback.com/
Save the Manatee Club **savethemanatee.org**

"Mother Nature knows that deep in our hearts we know too."

Wolves are extremely intelligent creatures with a highly evolved social structure. The entire pack is very loving toward the pups, helping to guide and guard them as they grow.

We can learn a lot from wolves about friendship, loyalty, cooperation and listening to the wisdom in our hearts when we need to make decisions that impact others in our "pack".
To read more about wolves in the wild visit
http://www.canadianwolfcoalition.com/

www.naturebooks4kids.com

"One touch of nature makes the whole world kin."

William Shakespeare